Where Did Mommy's Superpowers Go?

Helping Kids Understand
a Parent's Serious Illness

By
Jenifer
Gershman

Illustrated
By Randy
Jennings

Sweet Dreams Publishing
of Massachusetts

Where Did Mommy's Superpowers Go?

Cover Design: Randy Jennings
Interior Illustrations: Randy Jennings
Interior Layout: Susan Veach
Editorial and Proofreading: Eden Rivers Editorial Services

Published by Sweet Dreams Publishing of Massachusetts
36 Captain's Way
East Bridgewater, MA 02333

For more information about this book contact Lisa Akoury-Ross at Sweet Dreams
Publishing of MA by email at lross@PublishAtSweetDreams.com.

Library of Congress Control Number: 2010935008
ISBN-13: 978-0-9824461-9-5
Printed in the United States of America

Introduction

In 2007, at the age of 38, Jenifer Gershman was diagnosed with a rare and life-threatening bone marrow disease. In an instant, the fit and active young mother found herself facing a long hospitalization. To make matters worse, the aggressive treatment would require Jenifer to be separated from her four-year-old son, Jason, for weeks. Jenifer searched in vain for a book to help explain her anticipated absence, and to reassure Jason about the effects the treatment would have on her physical abilities and appearance. Unfortunately, the only books available described conditions different from her own. As a solution, Jenifer decided to create a book without a specific diagnosis and treatment. The story shows how talking openly and honestly with children when a parent is sick can minimize fear, and enhance their understanding. *Where Did Mommy's Superpowers Go?* is intended to support children who are coping with a seriously ill adult in their family, regardless of what the diagnosis may be, and is a useful tool in helping families prepare for this journey together.

A Note from the Author

I want to thank my publisher and friend, Lisa Akoury-Ross, for believing in this book and supporting me as a new author. Prior to meeting Lisa completely by chance, I had given up on ever seeing this story in print, and shelved the manuscript. With Lisa's expertise, encouragement, and patience, my story was transformed into a book that is even more special than I could have imagined.

I would like to thank the amazing team of talented people who improved my story tremendously and taught me so much. Lisa Ann Schleipfer, editor and owner of Eden Rivers Editorial Services, was instrumental in perfecting the writing, and Susan Veach, graphic designer, created a seamless layout, merging the text and artwork beautifully.

Of course no children's book would be complete (or nearly as fun!) without wonderful artwork. A very special thank you to my artist, Randy Jennings, who was just as personally invested as I was in creating the best illustrations possible. I greatly appreciate Randy's ability to translate my ideas onto paper, and to offer artistic solutions of his own when I had none. Watching the characters come to life was truly one of the most enjoyable aspects of making this book, and I am incredibly grateful for his experience and vision.

Acknowledgments

First and foremost, I'd like to thank Dr. Andrei Kouznetsov from the bottom of my heart. Without his knowledge and expertise, I may not have been properly diagnosed and treated, and this book may never have been written. I always will credit "Dr. K." with saving my life.

Many thanks to the amazing, dedicated, and caring team of doctors, nurses, and staff members at the Amyloid Research and Treatment Center, and at the Stem Cell Clinic at Boston Medical Center, for their superior level of care and compassion. I am deeply grateful for their commitment to ongoing research, and feel extremely blessed to have been treated by the leading amyloidosis experts in the world.

To my mother-in-law, "Nana Sue," who took on the daunting task of temporarily stepping into my shoes to care for Jason; Susan, you're the best! She did such a terrific job, I never once had to worry about him, which made it possible for me to focus all my energy on getting better. She didn't once flinch at the thick, pages-long "Instruction Manual" I left for her, and for that I am eternally thankful!

I would like to thank my parents for all of their help over the last several years. From taking care of Jason to transportation, grocery shopping, housework, cooking…they were pulled in every direction, and did it all selflessly and without complaint. They spent weekends with me in Boston, and chauffeured me to and from medical appointments, never needing anything more than a good meal as a "thank you!"

To my sister Michele, thank you for your support, encouragement, and especially for keeping me laughing through one of the most challenging times of my life. Having Michele by my side the day I shaved my head made that experience much less traumatic, and even fun, because she was there to keep me smiling.

I truly have the best, most generous and caring friends in the world, and without them would not have been able to get through my treatment as smoothly as I did. Despite being busy with their own families, they found the time to take me wig shopping, cook dinner for us several times a week, stock our freezer full of food, take Jason for play dates, help with transportation and errands, shower me with gifts and care packages to lift my spirits, and create a beautiful quilt to surround me with their love. They treated Jason as one of their own children, and knowing he was in good, safe hands, I only had to worry about getting healthy. I credit much of my recovery to these amazing women who are more than just friends, they are family.

And to Steven, my incredibly loving and devoted husband, my best friend, words cannot begin to express how grateful I feel to have such an amazing partner in my life and by my side. He always found the humor in any situation, and kept me laughing even at my most difficult moments. He took amazing care of me, and always made me feel like his wife, not a patient. Steve administered my complicated medication with the skill of a nurse, handled the cooking like a pro, and satisfied all of my unusual food cravings without an ounce of complaint. During this experience, I felt we were less "patient and caregiver" and more of a team facing this challenge together, hand in hand. Thank you, Steven, for your strength, commitment and love that were as instrumental in my healing as any medicine in the world.

To Jason, whose hugs, kisses and snuggles are the best medicine in the world.

And to Steven, who always, even in my worst moments, makes me feel like the most beautiful woman on the planet, no matter what.

Every morning, Mommy wakes me up with kisses and snuggles, and brings me orange juice, my favorite!

Mommy is silly and wakes up all my stuffed animals too. They hide under the blankets, so she looks for lumps and then gives them each kisses, one by one!

"Wake up, sleepyheads!" she says.

We go downstairs and have breakfast together.
I slide my chair right next to Mommy's.
Sometimes I even sit on her lap! I like the smell of her coffee.

After breakfast Mommy lets me watch my favorite cartoons. She likes them too!

Mommy and I *do a lot of cool stuff* together, like...

playing on the swing set...
swimming in the pool...

going for a bike or scooter ride
(Mommy runs next to me)...
or snuggling up with popcorn and a movie.

8

Mommy is really strong too. She…

gives me piggyback rides…
helps me dress up and fly like a superhero…
and when I'm sleepy, she swoops me up to bed.

One day Mommy says she has something important to discuss with me, so I climb onto her lap.

Mommy tells me that her doctor found some yucky stuff in her body that is making her feel sick.

She draws a picture to show me all the different cells in the blood. First she draws the "good guys"...

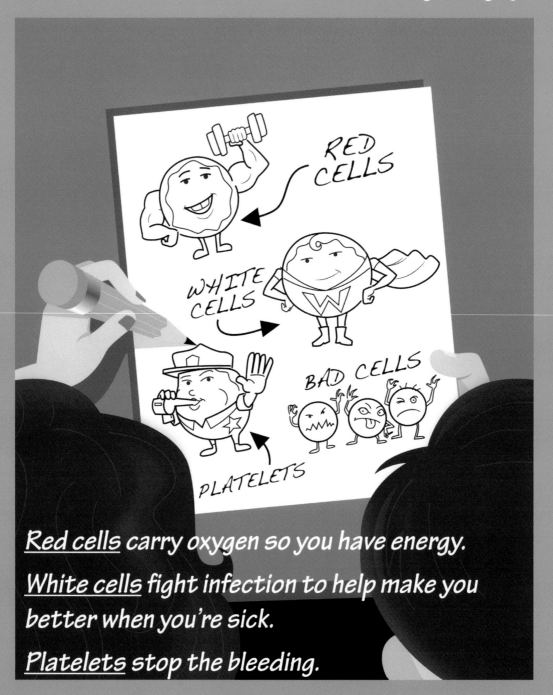

Red cells carry oxygen so you have energy.

White cells fight infection to help make you better when you're sick.

Platelets stop the bleeding.

and then she draws a ☹ to show the bad cells. I call these the "bad guys"!

Mommy says that she'll need very strong medicine to get rid of all the bad guys. But the medicine is so strong it will get rid of the good guys too!

"Without those good cells in my blood, I'll feel like a superhero without my superpowers for a little while," Mommy explains.

"Just like when a superhero gets caught in his enemy's trap?" I ask.

"Exactly!" Mommy says with a smile.

Without her superpowers, Mommy can get sick easily. She won't be able to push me on the swings, run next to my bike or scooter, take me swimming, give me piggyback rides, or help me fly like a superhero.

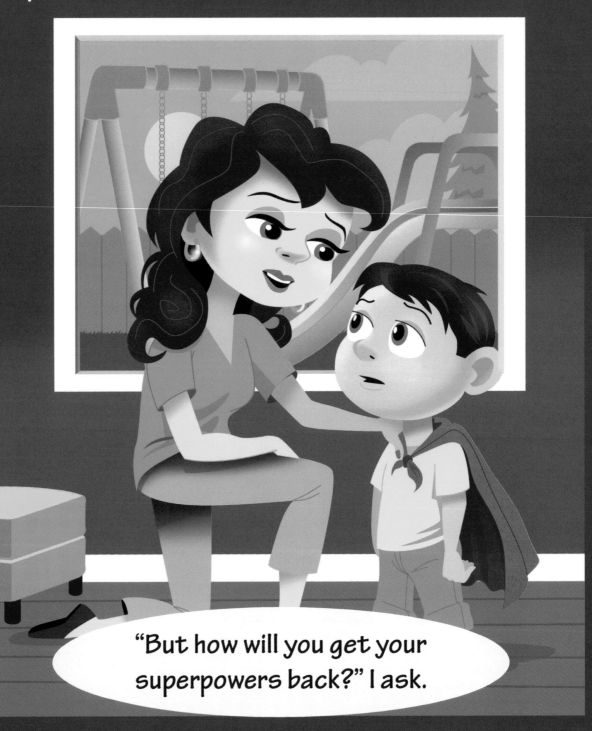

"But how will you get your superpowers back?" I ask.

"To get my superpowers back, the doctor will need to put new, healthy blood cells in my body," Mommy replies.

"As these baby cells grow and multiply, my superpowers will slowly come back and I will get stronger," she says with a smile.

Mommy tells me that after the treatment she will be very tired and weak for a while.

She will need to rest a lot, the way I do when I have a bad cold.

I'll need to remember to cover my mouth when I cough and sneeze, wash my hands a lot, and use "magic soap" to kill germs. I can do that!

Then Mommy says the strong medicine is so strong that it's going to make her long, curly hair fall out, and she's going to look just like me and Daddy.

I think it's cool that we'll all have matching haircuts!

Mommy tells me that she'll have to live near the hospital in a small apartment for a few weeks so the doctor can give her the strong medicine, and keep her safe from germs. I start to feel sad when I think of being apart from Mommy for so long.

"I have a great idea!" Mommy says. "Can you take care of something for me until I get back?" She gives me a special plant to take care of while she's gone. I can't wait to show Mommy what a good gardener I am when she comes home!

Mommy also tells me that without her superpowers, she'll be too weak and tired to drive or walk by herself. She will need Daddy to stay with her and help her get to the hospital every day. "Daddy will get to do the cooking, food shopping and laundry for *me* for a little while!" she laughs.

"Who will take care of me while you and Daddy are living near the hospital?" I ask.

"Nana is coming to stay at our house for as long as we need her," Mommy says.

I decide to give Mommy my stuffed puppy dog, Fondue, to take with her to the hospital. While Nana takes care of me, Daddy and Fondue will take care of Mommy at the hospital. Cuddling Fondue always makes me feel better, and I want Mommy to feel better too.

During the time Mommy is living near the hospital, we talk every day on the phone. I tell her all about my play dates, swimming lessons, and camp. She tells me how the doctors and nurses are taking such good care of her, and that Daddy is treating her like a princess! Then we give each other kisses over the phone.

Sometimes it's hard to stop talking and we don't want to say goodbye to each other, so it's more fun to race. We see who can be the first to hang up on "one … two … three!"

My other grandparents, Nonna and Pop-Pop, live nearby, and they come over a lot to play with me.

They take me to pick strawberries, ride the bumper boats, and see movies!

Daddy comes home to visit me on the weekends, and we spend lots of time together!

We ride bikes, go swimming, and even build model rockets! At bedtime, we snuggle and read together, but I wish Mommy could be here. "I miss Mommy," I tell him, with tears in my eyes. "She's been gone so long."

"She'll be home real soon, buddy, don't you worry," Daddy says and gives me a big hug in his strong arms. "The doctors are taking really good care of her."

One day Mommy calls to tell me the doctor said she can finally come home! I'm so excited to see her after all these weeks! Not all of her superpowers are back yet, but she has enough good guys in her blood to safely leave the hospital.

"Mommy will be home by the time we get back from the playground!" Nana tells me.

I can hardly wait!

When Nana and I come home from the park later that day, I run through the door and see Mommy sitting in a chair with her arms open for a huge hug! I fly into her lap and hug her so tight!

After lots of hugs and kisses, she says, "Do you want to see my funny hair? Daddy says it looks like a silly raccoon gave me a bad haircut!"

I notice she's wearing a scarf on her head, and wonder what Mommy looks like without her long curls.

"Okay," I answer.

She takes off her scarf, and her hair is short, fuzzy and messy; some spots don't have hair at all—she looks so funny! "Mommy, it *does* look like a silly raccoon gave you a bad haircut!"

We both laugh so hard!

Mommy tells me that her hair will grow back, and soon it will be just as long and curly as before. While she's waiting she'll wear a wig or scarves on her head.

"Would you like to help me pick out some pretty ones at the store?" she asks.

"Sure!" I answer.

Then Mommy tells me how very proud she is of me. She says I acted like a big boy, and thanks me for being so good for Nana.

Mommy says it was not easy to live away from me at the hospital. "I missed you every single second of every day!" she says.

I tell Mommy that I missed her too, and that I sometimes cried a little at night. "That's okay, honey," she says. "I cried too."

We hug each other so tight—I'm so glad she's finally home!

Mommy lets Fondue kiss my cheek, which tickles and makes me smile.

Even without her long curly hair, I can tell she's still the same silly Mommy I love!

Now Mommy has her superpowers back and is feeling great! We do our favorite things again, like...

playing on the swing set...
swimming in the pool...
going for a bike or scooter ride (Mommy still runs next to me)...

or snuggling up with popcorn and a movie.

And now that she has her superpowers back, Mommy is really strong too.

   She gives me piggyback rides…

   helps me dress up and fly like a superhero…

   and when I'm sleepy, swoops me up to bed!

Cartoon superheroes in movies and on TV are awesome and powerful, but Mommy will always be my real "Superhero"!

About the Author

Jenifer Gershman lives with her husband, Steven, and son, Jason, in Massachusetts. In 2007, at the age of 38, Jenifer was diagnosed with amyloidosis, a rare blood protein disorder which, left untreated, is fatal. Without prompt and proper treatment, the prognosis is approximately 12 to15 months. Jenifer underwent high dose chemotherapy and a stem cell transplant … TWICE … both in 2007 and 2008. Her son Jason was only 4 years old at the time of her first treatment. She is currently in remission and happy to be living a healthy and active life with her family.

For more information on amyloidosis and the Amyloid Research and Treatment Center at Boston Medical Center, please visit:

http://www.bu.edu/amyloid/

LaVergne, TN USA
16 March 2011
220428LV00002B